Fortune Tellers

by the Editors of Klutz

KLUTZ®

KLUTZ® creates activity books and other great stuff for kids ages 3 to 103. We began our corporate life in 1977 in a garage we shared with a Chevrolet Impala. Although we've outgrown that first office, Klutz galactic headquarters is still staffed entirely by real human beings. For those of you who collect mission statements, here's ours:

Create wonderful things • Be good • Have fun

Made in China. 68

©2022 Klutz. All rights reserved.

Distributed in the UK by
Scholastic UK Ltd
Euston House
24 Eversholt Street
London, NW1 1DB
United Kingdom

Distributed in the European Union by Scholastic Ltd
Unit 89E, Lagan Road
Dublin Industrial Estate
Glasnevin, Dublin 11
Ireland

Distributed in Australia by
Scholastic Australia Ltd
PO Box 579
Gosford, NSW
Australia 2250

Distributed in Hong Kong by
Scholastic Hong Kong Ltd
Suites 2001-2
Top Glory Tower
262 Gloucester Road
Causeway Bay, Hong Kong

Distributed in Canada by
Scholastic Canada Ltd
604 King Street West
Toronto, Ontario
Canada M5V 1E1

ISBN 978-1-338-79274-4
4 1 5 8 5 7 0 8 8

Write Us
We would love to hear your comments regarding this or any of our books.

KLUTZ®
557 Broadway
New York, NY 10012
thefolks@klutz.com

FSC
www.fsc.org
MIX
Paper from responsible sources
FSC® C135401

We make Klutz books using resources that have been approved according to the FSC® standard, which is managed by the Forest Stewardship Council®. This means the paper in this book comes from well managed FSC®-certified forests and other controlled sources.

Cover: p_jirawat/Shutterstock; Cover background & throughout: Mary Ne/Getty Images; 3 paper and throughout: Prasngkh Ta Kha/EyeEm/Getty Images; 8: Dziggyfoto/Getty Images; 51: Ardea-studio/Shutterstock; 69 top right: tatianazaets/Getty Images; 19, 20: discan/Getty Images; 61-68, 70: Ruslana_Vasiukova/Getty Images

Contents

What Is a Fortune Teller?

Behold, your future! Kids and grown-ups alike have been folding fortune tellers for years and years. (Ask your grandparents if they know what your fortune teller is!) With a pinch of your fingers, the folded paper can reveal deep mysteries of the universe . . . or just help you decide what sort of snack to eat.

Some folks call them cootie catchers and claim they'll scoop up any bad vibes, too.

Around the world, this nifty little contraption goes by different names: *piquito, flip-flapper, qua-qua, whirlybird, flexagon,* and *snapdragon* to name a few! What do you think a good name for this game would be?

How to Fold a Fortune Teller

Anyone can fold up a paper fortune teller lickety-split! (If you already know how to fold a fortune teller, feel free to skip this section.) Use one of the pages in this book, or any square piece of paper.

 1 Tear out one of the fortune teller pages. Place the paper face-down on a table. You should be looking at the dotted lines.

2 Fold the bottom right corner up to the top left corner diagonally, so you make a triangle. Crease the paper firmly.

 3 Unfold the paper. Then fold it diagonally the opposite way: bottom left corner to top right corner.

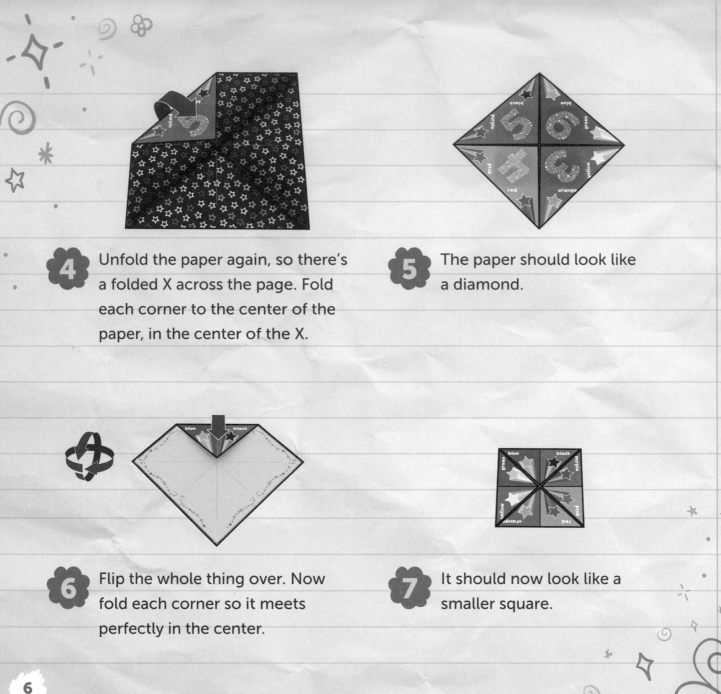

4 Unfold the paper again, so there's a folded X across the page. Fold each corner to the center of the paper, in the center of the X.

5 The paper should look like a diamond.

6 Flip the whole thing over. Now fold each corner so it meets perfectly in the center.

7 It should now look like a smaller square.

8 Fold the square in half from side to side.

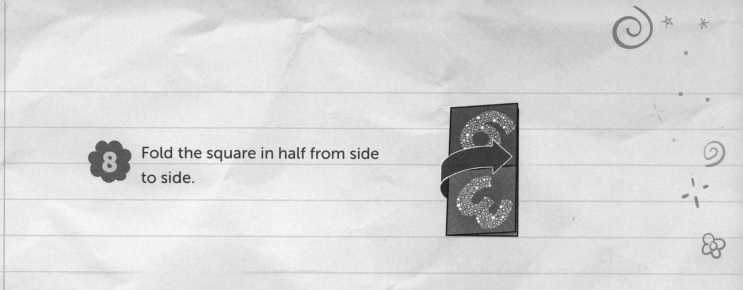

9 Unfold the square. Then fold it top to bottom.

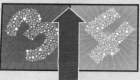

10 The last step needs you! Place each of your thumbs and index fingers in each pocket. Pinch your fingers to bring the corners together.

Now you're ready to play!

How to Play

Ask your friend to choose one of the corners. If the square has a number on it, open and close the fortune teller that many times. For example, if the number is 3, open and close the fortune teller three times.

Open up and down . . . ◀1▶

. . . side to side . . . ◀2▶

. . . up and down again. ◀3▶

WORDS OF WISDOM

If the corners have words, spell out the word. Or if it only has a color, spell out the color. For each letter, open and close the fortune teller. For example, if your word/color is "blue," open and close four times (one for each letter).

Open up and down. . . ◀B▶

. . . side to side. . . ◀L▶

. . . up and down. . . ◀U▶

. . . and side to side again. ◀E▶

If there's no number, word, or color, follow the game rules next to the fortune teller. Or, spell out your friend's name to find their fate!

2 After counting or spelling, freeze your fingers in place. Your friend picks one of the two triangles on the inside of the fortune teller.

3 Open and close the fortune teller depending on the number or spell out the word.

(If you don't see either, then spell out your friend's name!)

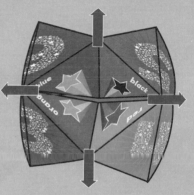

4 Time for your fortune! Your friend picks another triangle. Flip up the flap and read the fortune!

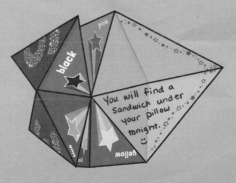

Who Are You?

Some fortune tellers reveal mesmerizing facts about yourself that maybe you didn't even know!

This is a paper fortune teller (cootie catcher).

Numbers on the flaps:
- 2
- 8
- 1
- 5

Animal labels:
- monkey
- zebra
- chameleon
- kangaroo
- lion
- cat
- owl
- squirrel

Fortunes inside:

You look best in black-and-white stripes.

You love to monkey around, no doubt about it.

When there's something important to do, you always hop to it.

Like a chameleon, you fit in just about anywhere.

People love to make you laugh, 'cause you always roar in delight.

People think you're the cat's meow.

You're so alert, it's like you have eyes in the back of your head.

At times, you can get pretty nutty!

SWOOSH!

3

BLAST!

4

Fiendish Genius
Your powers are in your head! With a brain that works at superhuman speeds, you have been known to outwit teachers and convince parents that candy is nutritious.

Wonder Toes
Your toes are where the power goes. You can tiptoe so softly that no one can hear you, wr te a book with your right foot, and dance on pointe like the star of the show.

Power Pink
Whenever you wear pink, you have superhero strength. You can run 10 miles without stopping, eat 100 cupcakes, and get your friends to do anything you want.

The Jokester
With your joking powers, you control all the laughs. You can cheer anyone up or save the day by making enemies laugh so hard, they cry.

VROOM!

7

POOF!

6

Souped-Up Super powers!

Find your superhero calling with the fortune teller on the page just before this one. Once you discover your superhero identity, draw a sketch of your supersuit here:

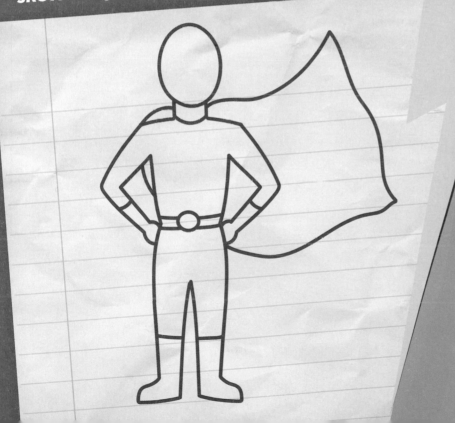

Find your superhero calling with the fortune teller on the page just before this one.

DOES YOUR SUPERHERO NEED A:

Cape?

Mask?

Shield?

Jetpack?

Secret identity?

Night-vision goggles?

Gloves or gauntlets?

Who is your sidekick?

_____

Who is your archnemesis (the villain or baddie)?

_____

BEST FRIENDS F♥REVER

Personalize a fortune teller for your friend!

1 Choose two words that describe your friend from the green box. Then choose *two words* each from the yellow, blue, and pink boxes.

Kind Stylish Bold Creative Cheerful	Smart Cool Gutsy Witty Silly
Unique Generous Athletic Positive Strong	Funny Talented Tough Sweet Brave

2 Write the words on the eight *colorful* triangles around the edge of the fortune teller. Write two words each in the green, blue, yellow, and pink triangles. If the triangles are already filled in, skip to Step 3.

3 Now write your friend's fortunes on the eight white *inner* triangles. Think about things, activities, or people they like. If giraffes are their favorite animal, a good fortune might be: "Tonight, you will dream about meeting a talking giraffe." Flip to page 29 if you need ideas for fortunes!

4 When you've filled in the blanks, tear out the fortune teller and fold it.

5 Now dazzle your friend with your predictions for the future. After you play, give your friend the fortune teller to keep.

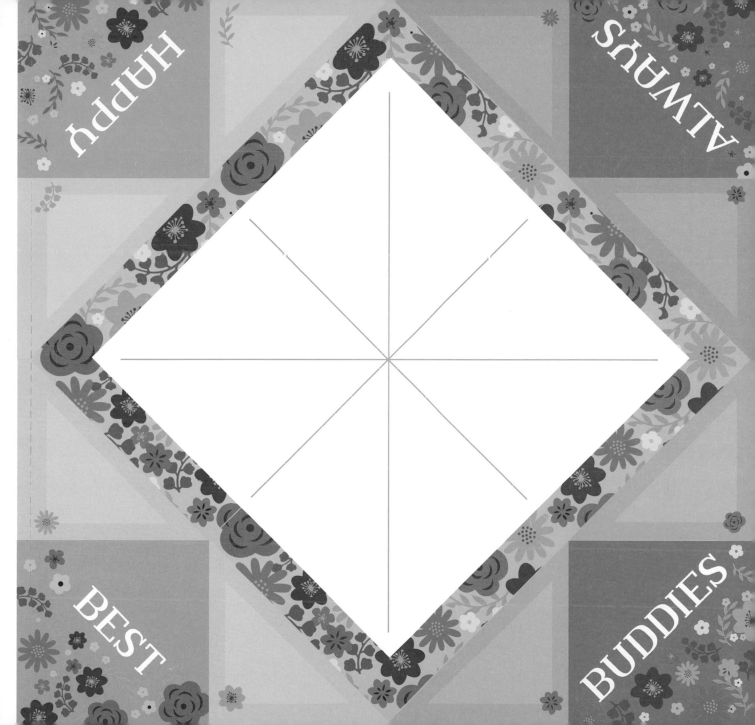

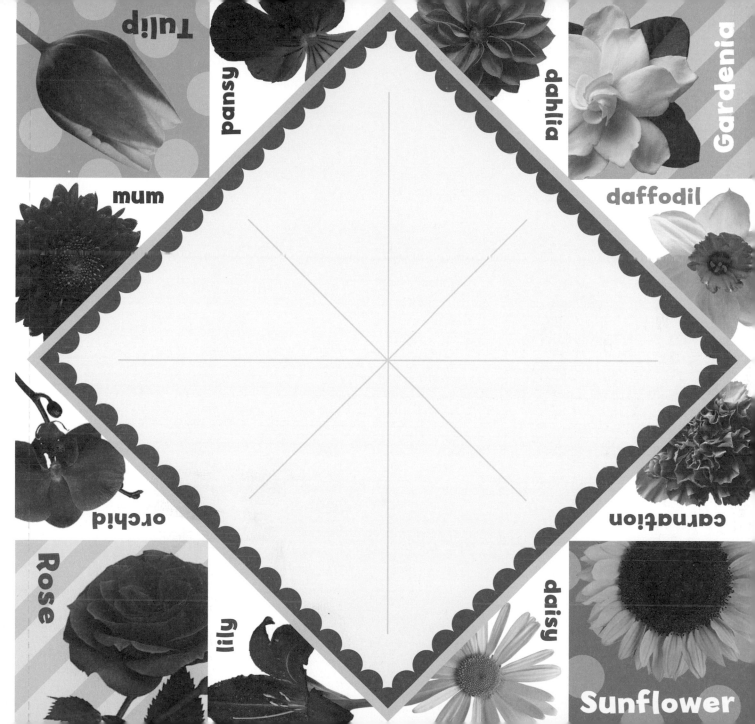

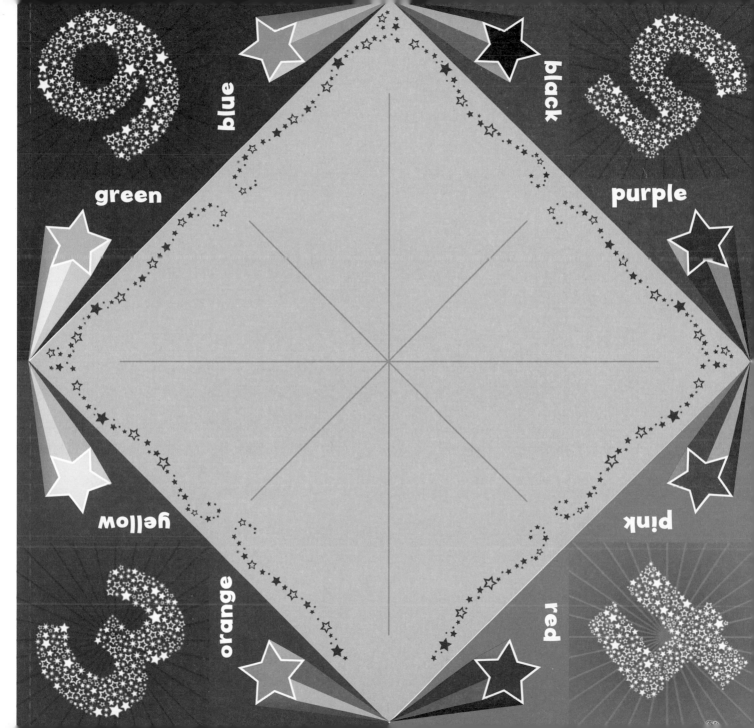

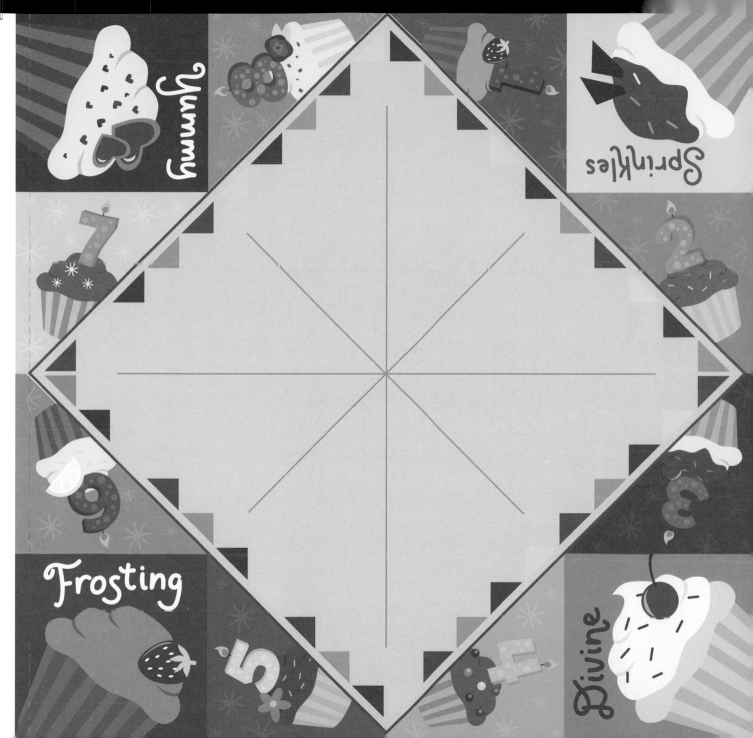

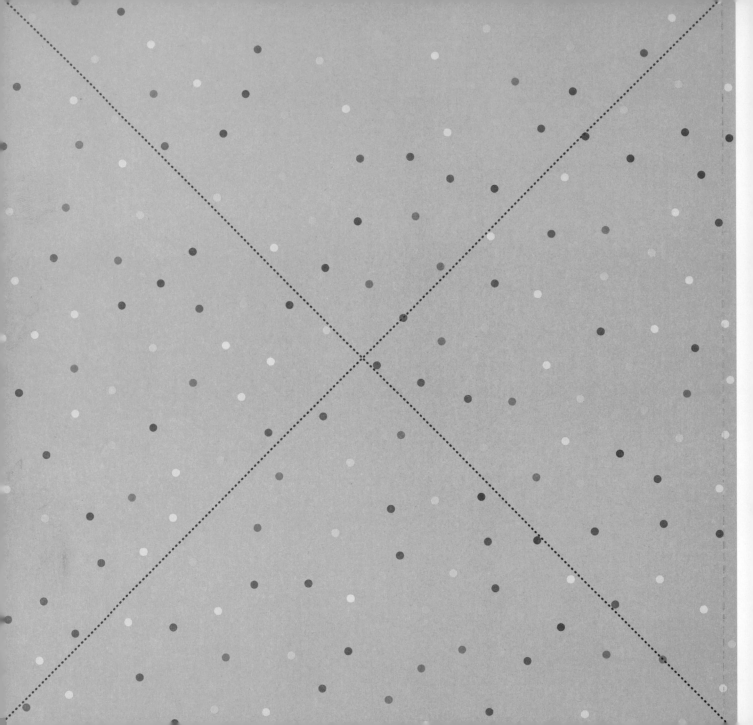

FEELING STUCK IN THE PRESENT?

Sometimes the future is a little hard to imagine. If you need some inspiration, here are fortunes you can borrow!

Looking for Advice?

Honesty is the solution to every problem.

Helping others is the surest path to happiness.

If you believe in unicorns, then they will believe in you!

Moving to Motivate?

Your hard work will pay off. Trust me: I'm a fortune teller.

Let your dreams fly as high as the clouds.

You are MAGIC. Don't let anyone dull your sparkle.

Need a Bit of Luck?

If the last word you say before you fall asleep tonight is rabbit, you'll have good luck tomorrow.

Write your birthdate in numbers and add them all together. That's your lucky number!

Wear something in your favorite color every day for the next week to get good vibes.

Feeling Funny?

I see something sweet in your future. It might be ice cream . . . or a monster made of marshmallows.

Be like a frog. They eat whatever bugs 'em.

Make like a berry and jam out to your favorite song.

Crystal Ball

Get a peek into your future. Find out the fate that awaits you, and predict your destiny.

 1 Carefully tear out and fold one of the next five fortune tellers.

2 Ask your friend to pick out a word from the corners. Open and close the fortune teller as you spell it out.

3 Now open and close the fortune teller as you spell out your friend's name.

 4 If you're using the billiards ball page, tell your friend to ask a question about their future. It can be any question that can be answered with "yes" or "no."

5 Ask your friend to pick a word or color from the inner corners. Flip up the flap. The answer to their question is underneath!

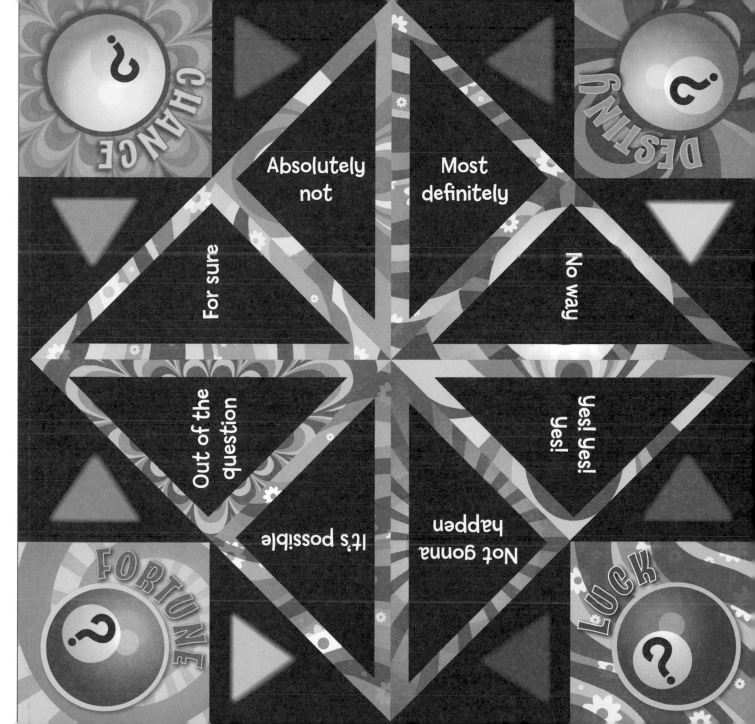

SCREAM

SCREECH

CAT

SPOOKY

SKELETON

13

JINX

To scare off evil spirits, hop on one foot and say "hippopotamus" 12 times.

If you say the word "I" in the next five minutes, you'll have bad luck for a week.

Your future BFF will be revealed to you in a dream.

Someone will tell you a secret in the near future. Sh‑h– don't tell!

Your closet is haunted by the ghosts of stinky socks.

CLOSET

The next song you hear will be a message from the spirits.

CURSE

Don't look in the mirror tonight–or you'll be visited by a glass ghost!

The next teacher you will see is secretly a vampire.

HAUNT

HOUSE

EVIL

GLOW

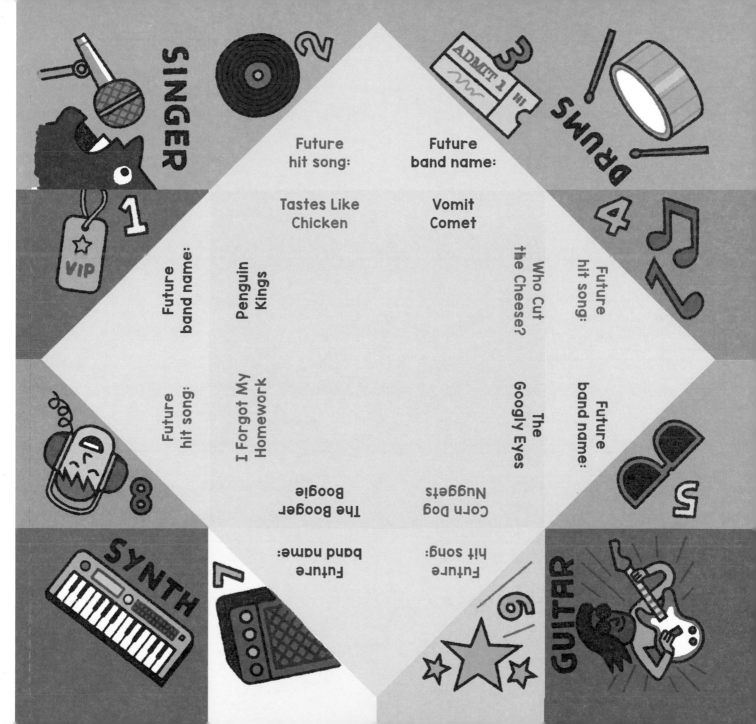

swim

Star

Champ

shoot

kick

flip

By the time you get to high school, you'll be able to dunk.

You'll set a world record in every swimming event, never to be beaten.

You'll score the gold-medal goal for the Olympic soccer team.

Time to tumble: You're going to win a gold for all-around gymnastics.

Get your racket ready because you're going to dominate the U.S. Open.

You'll hit so many home runs you'll be inducted into the Hall of Fame.

Your amazing jumping skills will make you a beach volleyball pro.

You're going to race your way to the top as a track and field superstar.

serve

throw

Pro

spike

sprint

Winner

FIND YOUR GOOD LUCK CHARM!

Surround yourself with good thoughts, and good luck is sure to find you. What kind of charm will bring you the best luck? Take this quiz, then add up your points at the end to find out!

At my slumber party, my friends and I will definitely:

A. Make ice cream sundaes
B. Build a blanket fort
C. Watch a sappy movie
D. Stay up all night

My favorite color is:

A. Green
B. Red
C. Yellow
D. Pink

The best kind of cake is:

A. Coconut-lemon
B. Red velvet
C. Carrot cake
D. Confetti sprinkles

If I could make one wish come true, it would be to:

A. Go on a magical adventure
B. Have superpowers
C. Help animals in need
D. Win a sports championship

My perfect day would have a:

A. Nature walk
B. Picnic in the park
C. Pony ride
D. Roller coaster

Add up the answers, and follow the key to find your lucky trinket!

For every A answer, give yourself 1 point.

For every B answer, give yourself 2 points.

For every C answer, give yourself 3 points.

For every D answer, give yourself 4 points.

Four-Leaf Clover (5-8 points)
You're one in a million! Keep a lookout for this plucky, lucky leaf.

Ladybug (9-12 points)
Sweet and sassy, this lovely bug is a sign of good things to come.

Shiny Horseshoe (13-16 points)
Giddy-up for good fortune! You are a loyal friend who looks after those around you.

Fuzzy Dice (17-20 points)
You have an adventurous spirit, and like to roll with the action. Your future looks bright!

Truth or Dare

Share a secret, or do something silly! The future is in the fortune teller, but the choice is yours!

If your friend doesn't answer the truth or dare, they have to say one nice thing about you instead.

 1 Choose one of the next three pages. If it's blank, fill in your own "truth" questions on the blue triangles. Fill in "dare" prompts on the green squares. If it's already filled in, just skip to the next step.

 2 Fold up your fortune teller and place it on something smooth like a table or the top of a book.

 3 Give the fortune teller a spin, until it stops or your friend says "STOP!"

 4 Pick up the fortune teller. Open and close it as you spell out your friend's name.

 5 Ask your friend to pick a truth-or-dare triangle. Flip up the flap. If they chose truth, they answer the question. If they chose dare, they do the dare!

truth

dare

truth

dare

truth

dare

truth

dare

Sing a song to the person next to you.

Truth Transfer! Ask the person next to you any question you want.

What's the weirdest dream you've ever had?

Show off your best dance moves!

Make the silliest face you can.

Have you ever had an imaginary friend?

If you were stuck on a deserted island, who would you most want to be stuck with?

Smell your socks!

HUNGRY

DARE

TRUTH

YUMMY

TRUTH

DARE

Squaaawk! Act like a chicken for one minute.

If you found a hundred dollars on the ground, would you keep it?

Do you have a hidden talent?

Make up a rap about your underpants!

What nickname do you wish you had?

Laugh like a hyena for one minute.

If you could switch lives with someone for one day, who would it be?

Do as many push-ups as you can.

TRUTH

DARE

TRUTH

LUNCH

TRUTH

DARE

SNACKS

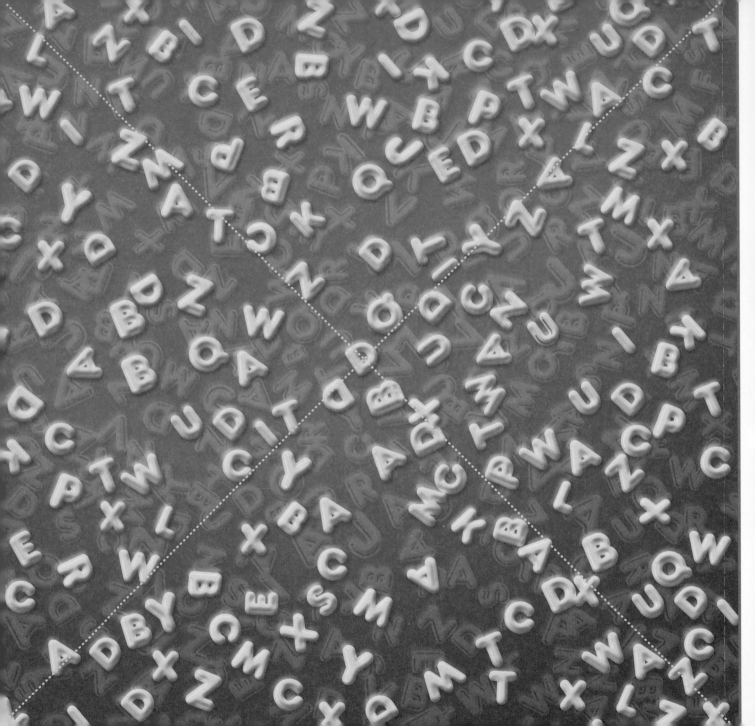

THE ULTIMATE TRUTH-OR-DARE LIST

Need some help thinking of answers to your truth-or-dare fortune tellers? Here are the best (not-mean) questions and dares to try.

Truth

What character from a book would you most want to be?

If you had a unicorn, what would you name it?

What's your favorite thing to daydream about?

Have you ever slept in late? If so, what's the latest time you ever woke up?

Are you a cat person or a dog person?

Do you believe in aliens?

What's the silliest thing in your room?

Who's the funniest person you know?

Are you ticklish? If so, where are you the *most* ticklish?

What grosses you out more than anything in the whole world?

Would you rather have pink, blue, green, or purple hair?

If you were a food, what type of food would you be and why?

Dare

Read the entire credits out loud at the end of your next movie night.

Sing whatever song the fortune teller holder requests.

Pretend to be a cooking-show host who is making your friends a snack.

Keep a serious face for one minute while your friend tries to make you laugh.

Talk like a pirate for the next 5 minutes.

Howl like a werewolf during a full moon.

Wear your socks on your hands for the next 5 minutes.

Smell your shirt and describe what it smells like.

Try to touch your tongue to your nose.

Create a fun nickname for everyone in the room.

Tell your favorite toy that you love them.

Walk to the other side of the room and back like you're on a fashion runway.

M.A.S.H. Remix

Kids have been playing M.A.S.H. since (almost) the beginning of time! This game is easy to play with fortune tellers, too.

 1 Tear out the next three pages. If it's blank, you'll need to fill it in with answers to these questions:

1. Where will I live?
2. What kind of job will I do?
3. What sort of pet will I have?
4. What kind of car will I drive?

Flip to page 57 if you need help with ideas to write on your fortune teller.

 2 Fold up your fortune teller and place it on something smooth like a table or the top of a book.

 3 Your friend picks just **one** question to answer. **Give the fortune teller a spin,** until it stops or your friend says "STOP!"

 4 Pick up the fortune teller. Open and close it as you spell out your friend's name.

 5 Have your friend pick a triangle. Flip up the flap to reveal their destiny!

1. Fancy townhouse in Paris
2. Soccer superstar
3. Tropical fish
4. A brand-new SUV

1. Tent on a tropical beach
2. Chef
3. A 200-pound dog
4. Cherry red convertible

1. Cabin in the woods
2. Doggie daycare owner
3. Three cats
4. Wood-paneled station wagon

1. Next door to your best friend
2. Wrecking ball operator
3. A pug
4. The same car as your grandma.

M.A.S.H. Story Starter

Need some help figuring out funny answers to your M.A.S.H. fortune tellers? Here's an easy way to get started!

1
Without showing your friend the story, ask her to come up with a word for each box.

2
After you fill in all the boxes, read the story out loud.

3
Now copy your friend's answers into the matching boxes on one of the blank M.A.S.H. fortune tellers. For example, if you write "pink poodle" in the orange box, write "pink poodle" in one of the orange boxes on the fortune teller.

4
Your M.A.S.H. fortune teller is ready. Time to get mashing!

THE QUEST OF A LIFETIME

Being adventurers was even better than

_____ and _____
[your name]   [your friend's name]

thought. Fame and fortune at the age of 12—who could ask for more? Ever since they had met the talking

_____ who had gifted them the flying
[magical creature]

_____, the friends had traveled the
[form of transportation]

world to such exciting places as

_____ and _____.
[country]   [country]

Every day, they got letters asking for help. So far, they had helped a _____ recover their lost
[job]

_____, and a _____ find their
[fancy car]   [job]

_____ that had run away with their best
[zoo animal]

friend, a _____ to _____.
[type of pet]   [country]

They had even uncovered a _____ haunted
[form of transportation]

by ghosts in _____.
[your hometown]

One day, their archnemesis, the evil

_____, sent a _____ to
[color + animal]   [job]

deliver a message to them that would turn into the question of a lifetime.

"Dear _____ and _____,
[your name]   [your friend's name]

If you ever want to see your precious _____,
[your family's car]

you must deliver one million dollars to the secret agent

who is disguised as a _____. It's your
[job]

move . . . "

57

Letter to My Future Self

A letter to your future self is like a little time capsule. You can write a letter to yourself whenever you want!

First, tear out one of the following pieces of paper. Write a letter addressed "Dear me" or use your name. Your letter can be as short or as long as you like.

What is your life like now?

What do you hope you are doing in the future?

What do you hope you have learned?

Got your letter written?
It's time to seal up your time capsule!

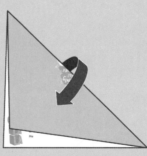

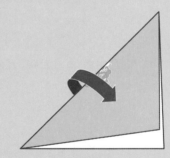

 Put your letter on the table, with the letter side facing up. Fold the paper diagonally, bringing the upper right corner down to the lower left corner.

 Unfold the paper. You'll see a crease where you made the fold.

 Fold the paper again diagonally, in the opposite way. Upper left corner down to bottom right corner.

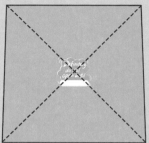

  Unfold.

 Now fold the paper in half, top to bottom.

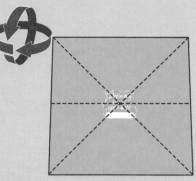

 Open the page and flip it over, so you're looking at the back of the paper.

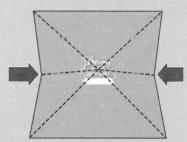

 Push in on the little triangles on the sides.

 As you push, the paper will fold in on itself so that a triangle begins to form. Press down to create the triangle.

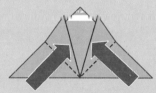

 Lift up the left and right corners. Fold them up toward the center. This makes a tiny diamond shape.

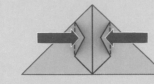

 10 Fold the left and right points of the diamond so the points meet in the middle.

11 Fold the two tips down on the top layer of the diamond.

 12 Tuck the loose top of the diamond down and into the little flaps.

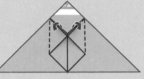

 13 Flip the triangle over and repeat. Once you're done, it will look like a squashed hexagon.

14 Write today's date on the outside. Fill in a date when you want to open your letter. It could be on your birthday, a year from now, ten years from now, or whenever you want. Do not peek until the date on your time capsule arrives!

If you blow into the hole at the top of the diamond, the time capsule will inflate! If someone asks, tell them it's full of secrets!

Long Time No See (Me!)

Hey there, _____ !
[your name]

Wow, it's been a minute, hasn't it? If you opened this letter on the right date, it's been _____ days/months/years since you (er, I mean
[fill in the number]   [circle one]
since we) wrote this letter.

As of writing, I am _____ years old. It's the oldest I've ever been!
[fill in the number]

In the future (which is your "now") I hope you are doing this:

_____

_____

_____
[fill in your hopes and dreams for your future self]

Here are some things I hope you don't forget about when you're older:

_____

_____

_____
[fill in the best stuff about now]

Well, that's all for now! Write me back!*

Stay cool,

_____
[your name, again]

To: Future
Me

DO NOT OPEN UNTIL:

A DAY IN THE LIFE

It's pretty neat to be me! Here's everything I did on _____.
[today's date]

I woke up at:

For breakfast I ate:

In the morning I did this:

For lunch I ate:

In the afternoon I did this:

For dinner I ate:

In the evening I did this:

I went to bed at:

Best Stuff Ever

The things you like can change over time. Do you think you will like the same things when you read this letter later?

	Now	Later
My favorite food is:		
My favorite book is:		
My favorite movie is:		
My best friend is:		
My favorite class or teacher is:		
Here's the best joke I know:		
This song is my jam:		
If I could wish for one thing, it would be this:		

Blast From the Past

Dear Me,

In case you forget what life was like in the **year** _____,
[what year it is now]
here's what's on my mind in this exact moment,

_____.
[today's date and time]

My favorite thing about my **home** is this: _____.
In my free time, my **favorite hobby** or thing to do is this: _____.

What I like about school the most is: _____.
My **not-so-favorite thing** about school is: _____.

The **best thing** about my life right now is: _____.
The **worst thing** about my life right now is: _____.

One thing on **everybody's mind** right now is this: _____.
Here's **what I think** about it: _____.

Hope that was an interesting trip down memory lane. Why not write another letter to your future self about what's on your mind right now?

Sincerely yours,
Me

today's
date _____

Time Capsule

OH
LA
LA

Read Your Palm

Today's date:

Today's weather:

My mood:

My favorite thing:

Hi,
__-year-old
me!

Draw a self-portrait.